Hatshepsut
First Female Pharaoh

Shirley J. Jordan, M.S.

Publishing Credits

Content Consultant
Blane Conklin, Ph.D.

Associate Editor
Christina Hill, M.A.

Assistant Editor
Torrey Maloof

Editorial Assistants
Deborah Buchanan
Kathryn R. Kiley
Judy Tan

Editorial Director
Emily R. Smith, M.A.Ed.

Editor-in-Chief
Sharon Coan, M.S.Ed.

Editorial Manager
Gisela Lee, M.A.

Creative Director
Lee Aucoin

Cover Designer
Lesley Palmer

Designers
Deb Brown
Zac Calbert
Amy Couch
Robin Erickson
Neri Garcia

Publisher
Rachelle Cracchiolo, M.S.Ed.

Teacher Created Materials
5301 Oceanus Drive
Huntington Beach, CA 92649-1030
http://www.tcmpub.com
ISBN 978-0-7439-0429-2

Table of Contents

Hatshepsut: The Female Pharaoh

Many people have called Hatshepsut (hat-SHEP-soot) the greatest woman in Egypt's history. She lived during the years historians call the New Kingdom.

Before her time, no woman had ever ruled Egypt. Hatshepsut's father was Thutmose I (THUHT-mohs). When he died, there was no son in direct line to become **pharaoh** (FAIR-o). So, Hatshepsut became an important part of Egypt's history. Sometimes, she shared the throne with her husband. At other times, she ruled alone. Hatshepsut brought energy and wisdom to almost 20 years of Egypt's history.

The Rosetta Stone ▼

Knowing the Date

The time of ancient Egypt lasted for nearly 3,000 years. This history was so long ago that people who study it sometimes cannot agree what year a certain thing happened.

Reading the Rosetta Stone

In 1799, a great discovery was made. An **artifact** (AWR-tih-fact) called the Rosetta Stone was found. This stone was the key to understanding Egypt's language. Once you know the language, you can learn more about a **civilization** (siv-uh-luh-ZAY-shuhn).

▼ The Nile River was important to life in ancient Egypt.

A Royal Birth

Hatshepsut was born around 1508 B.C. Her family was the most important family in Egypt. A man named Thutmose I was her father. He was the pharaoh. That means he was the ruler of the whole country.

Thutmose I had more than one wife. The first one, the great queen, was Queen Ahmose (AH-mohs). She was Hatshepsut's mother.

Hatshepsut had two brothers and one sister, but none of them lived to be adults. She knew her father must have missed his sons. So, she sometimes wore boys' clothing to make him feel better.

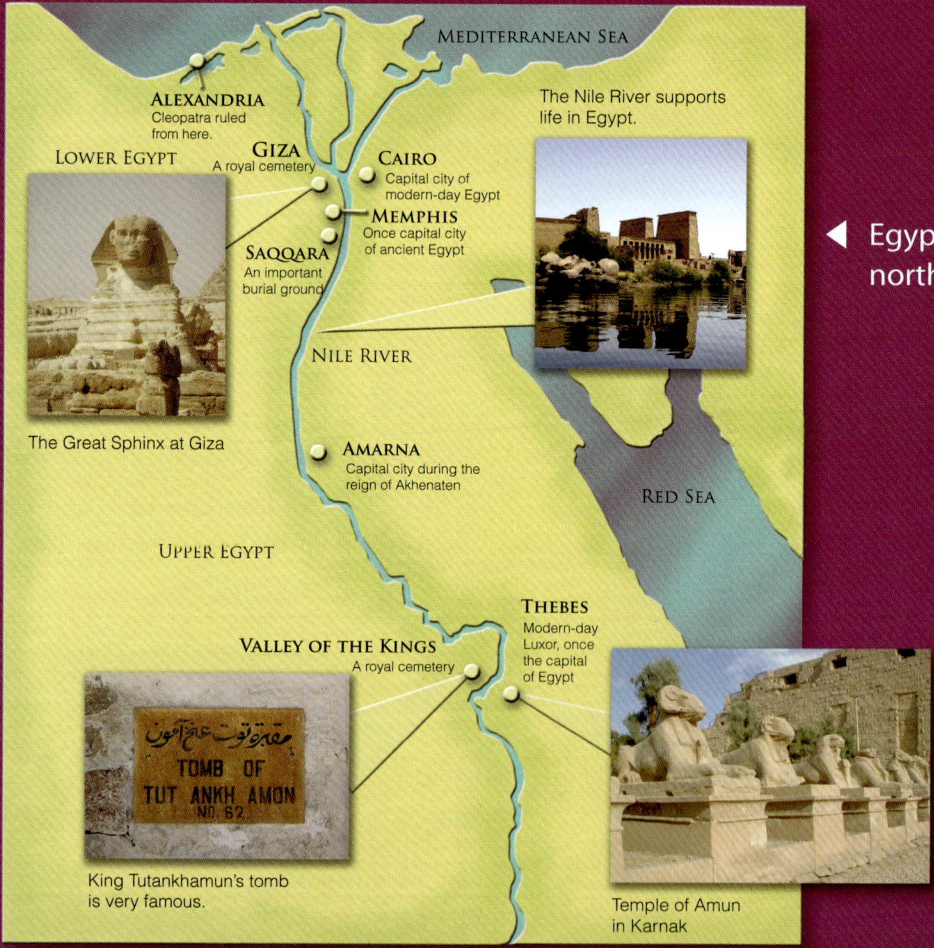

Egypt is in northeastern Africa.

◀ Ancient Thebes was an important city. Today, people visit the city's ruins.

Happy Parents

In other ancient cultures like the Romans, Greeks, and Hebrews, sons were considered much more important than daughters. The Egyptians were more like families today. They welcomed the birth of both boys and girls.

Thebes Today

The city of Thebes is known today as Luxor (LUKS-ore).

Life for a pharaoh's daughter was a happy one. She had plenty to eat and many servants. The royal family lived in a fine palace in Egypt's capital, Thebes (THEEBZ).

▲ Luxor today

An Empty Throne

When Hatshepsut was a teenager, her father died. With Thutmose I gone, who would rule Egypt? Even though Egyptian girls and women had many rights, the pharaoh had always been a man. Would the Egyptians allow a young woman to rule them?

Hatshepsut was a strong young woman who wanted to lead others. She could read and write. And, she liked to learn new things. She had watched her father while he ruled as pharaoh. Hatshepsut had many ideas about how to make Egypt great.

There are sculptures and carvings showing what Hatshepsut looked like.

▲ Pharaohs in Egypt had more than one wife.

Thutmose I had a son. However, the boy was not in line to be the new pharaoh. His mother was not the pharaoh's first wife. The son's name was Thutmose II, and he was about eight years old. He was Hatshepsut's half brother. They had the same father but different mothers.

Young Hatshepsut had advisors to help her. They had an idea. If she married her half brother, she and Thutmose II could rule Egypt together!

Many Wives

In ancient days, a man could be married to several wives at one time. He usually did this so he would have children still living after his death. Today, there are better medicines, and most children grow up healthy. Modern laws limit marriages in this country. Each person can only be married to one person at a time.

Marriages Between Relatives

It was common in ancient times for brothers and sisters to marry. In those times, the people believed this made a ruling family more powerful. Today, scientists know that the children from such marriages can have health problems.

A Royal Wedding

Hatshepsut and her young half brother were married. Thutmose II, who was still a young boy, became the pharaoh. Hatshepsut was his **regent** (REE-juhnt). A regent is someone who rules when the real leader is too young or too ill to lead alone. She made many important decisions for Egypt.

Historians cannot agree on the ages of Hatshepsut and Thutmose II. When her father died, Hatshepsut was probably somewhere between 12 and 17 years old. Most historians think her half brother was seven years younger.

Thutmose II grew up to be a weak man. He was not a leader like his father. Scientists used X-rays to study the **mummy** of Thutmose II. Using X-rays means they do not damage the mummy. They learned a lot about Thutmose II from looking at his X-rays.

▲ Scientists study mummies to learn about life in ancient Egypt.

▲ Egyptologist Howard Carter examines a mummy.

How Rulers Are Numbered

Once the first Thutmose had a son, the father was called Thutmose I. This way, people knew who was being spoken about. Hatshepsut's husband was named Thutmose II (the second). Later, Thutmose II had a son who was Thutmose III (the third).

An Unusual Hair Style

Most pharaohs have been pictured as bald or with little hair. Thutmose II had very long hair. **Egyptologists** (ee-jip-TAWL-uh-jistz) think he had his servants curl it with a device much like today's curling irons.

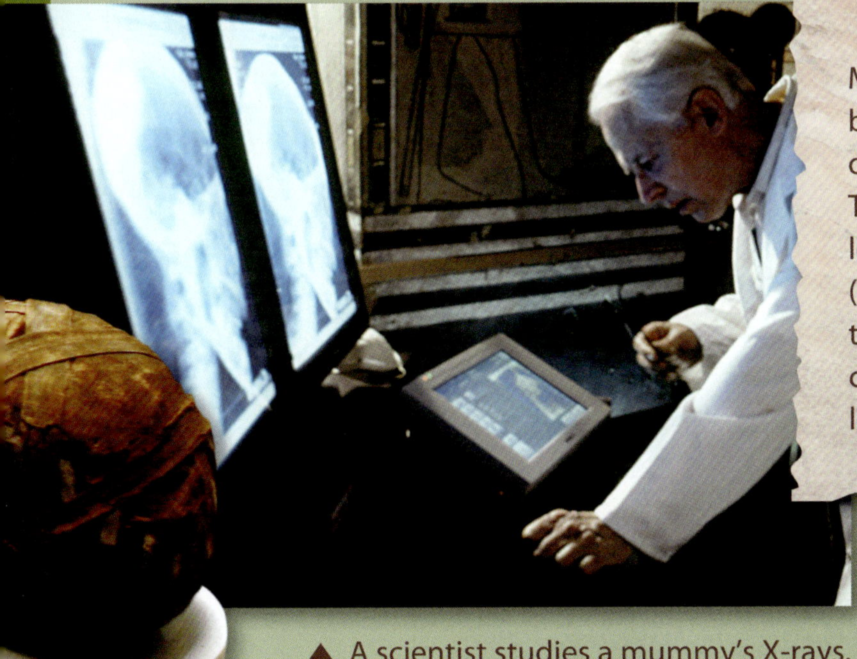

▲ A scientist studies a mummy's X-rays.

The Power Behind the Throne

Thutmose II was the pharaoh. And, Hatshepsut was only his regent. But, she was really the person who led Egypt through some of its best years. Drawings of them show her walking and standing behind her husband. She was giving him the respect a pharaoh deserved.

Hatshepsut was very strong willed and intelligent. In fact, she was smarter than Thutmose II. She was definitely in better health. She made most of the decisions about the nation. The priests and other leaders of Egypt followed her advice.

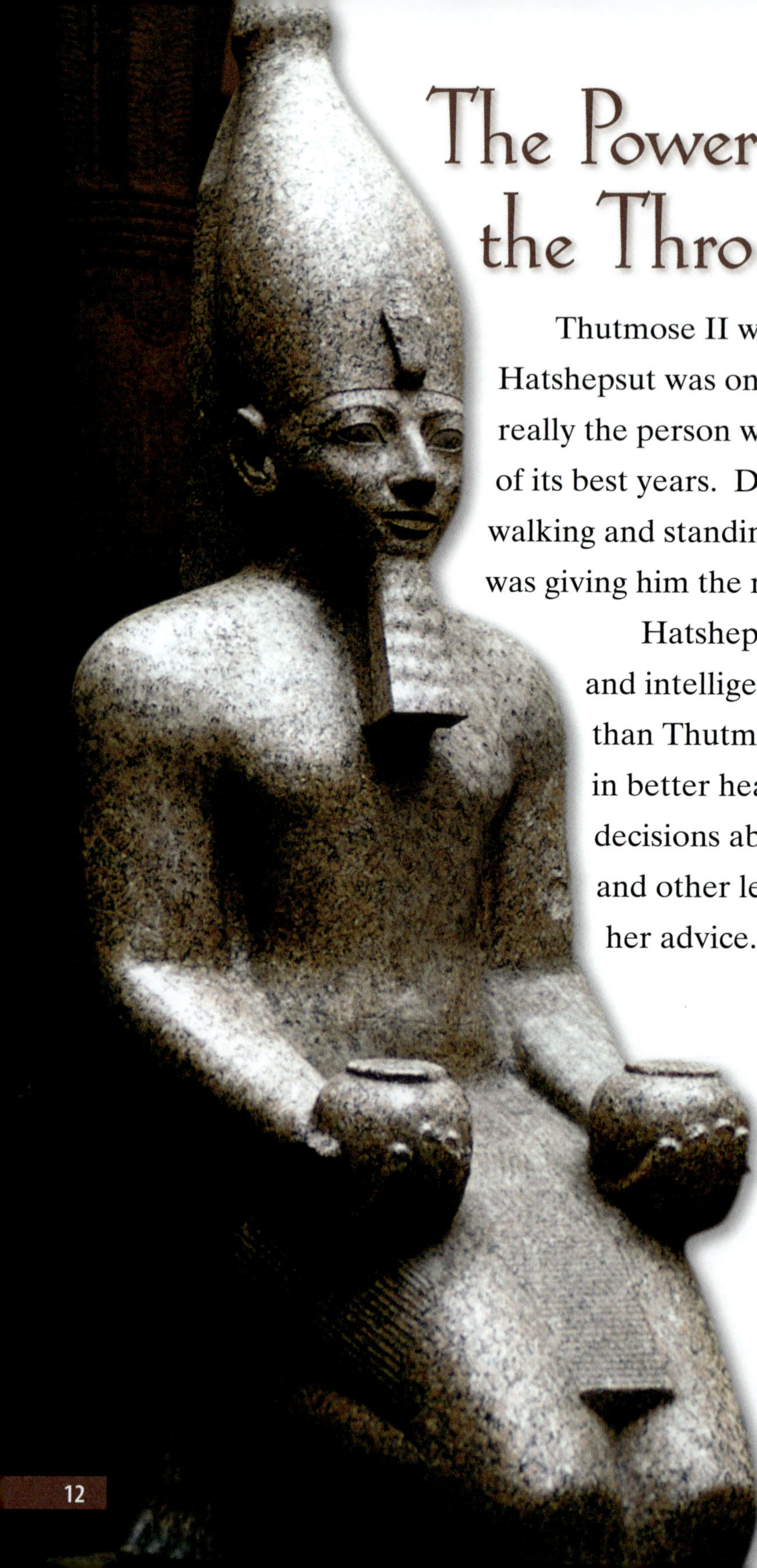

◀ Hatshepsut

▲ These are hieroglyphs on a wall in Egypt.

Soon, they had a daughter. Her name was Princess Neferure (neh-fuhr-OOH-ruh). The daughter of a pharaoh was usually raised to become the wife of the next pharaoh. But, there are signs that Hatshepsut was also teaching her daughter how to run a country.

The Scribes

The Egyptians honored people who had learned to read and write. These men were called **scribes**. They wrote down important facts. They had to know almost 700 symbols to represent words. These symbols are called **hieroglyphs** (HI-ruh-glifs).

The Job of the Pharaoh

A pharaoh needed many powerful people to help run Egypt. There were priests and generals. There were also rich people who owned a lot of land. The pharaoh was careful to make sure that these people approved all important decisions.

Another Pharaoh

Thutmose II ruled for about 10 years with Hatshepsut as his regent. Hatshepsut probably hoped that Princess Neferure would have an important role in the government. She was often seen in public. She was not as powerful as her mother. But, she was expected to marry the next pharaoh. Unfortunately, this was a role she would never play. She died before a marriage could be arranged.

Thutmose II was still a young man when he died. The throne was empty again. Thutmose II had had a son with another woman. His name was Thutmose III. In about 1504 B.C., Thutmose III became pharaoh.

▲ These hieroglyphs represent Thutmose II and Hatshepsut.

▲ Farming was important in ancient Egypt.

The new pharaoh was only a young baby. Again Hatshepsut became the regent. She was now in her twenties. How angry she must have been! She was sharing power with a baby. However, she accepted her role, just as she had before.

Life for the Egyptian

During the years that Hatshepsut was regent, life was good for Egyptians. There were many crops. Barley, onions, beans, and wheat grew well in the lands by the Nile River. Cattle, goats, and sheep were raised for food. The Egyptians also hunted antelopes, wild oxen, rabbits, wolves, and leopards.

Trading Goods

Hatshepsut wanted peace with other countries. She believed trade was more important than fighting over land. The Egyptians did not spend money for goods. Instead, they traded goods back and forth.

The Nile River made trading in ancient Egypt easier. ▶

Hatshepsut Takes the Throne

Hatshepsut had been regent for about seven years. More and more, her power had grown. The priests and other leaders followed her orders. As time passed, she gradually became the only one who made decisions. Thutmose III faded farther and farther into the background at the palace.

In about 1473 B.C., Hatshepsut declared herself pharaoh. She took the throne. Now, she had full power as ruler over all of Egypt. This meant that the **double crown** of the pharaoh was hers. Egypt's pharaohs wore a double crown. Half of the crown was white. That stood for the south (Upper Egypt). The other half was red. It represented the north (Lower Egypt). The full crown meant that the two parts of Egypt were all part of one country.

As pharaoh, Hatshepsut made Egypt more beautiful. She ordered the walled gardens of the royal palace planted with flowers. And, other rare plants were brought from Asia.

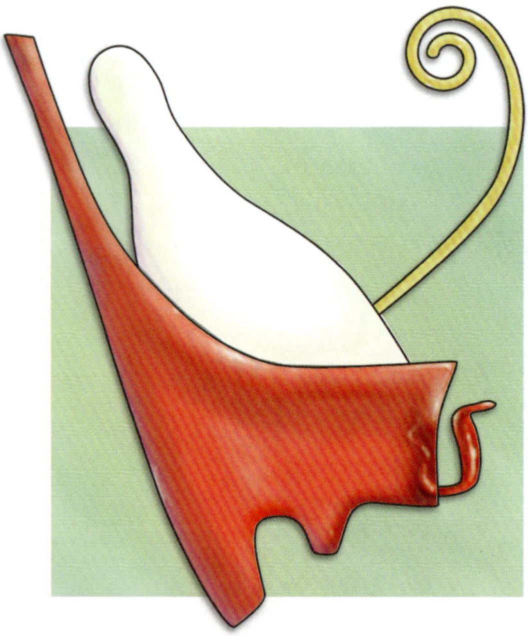

▲ The double crown was worn by Hatshepsut.

Much of what is known about Egypt is learned from wall carvings or paintings.

Where Was Thutmose?

Some Egyptologists think that young Thutmose III was afraid of Hatshepsut's power. Others believe he was away with Egypt's army. Wall paintings have been found that show him leading the army in battle.

Royal Buildings

The pharaoh's palace was large and beautiful. But, its walls were like those of regular houses. The walls were made with bricks. The bricks were dried mud, water, and reeds. Over the bricks was plaster to make them stronger. Only Egypt's royal pyramids and tombs were cut from stone.

"His" Majesty Rules

Hatshepsut was a powerful ruler. The priests and other important men respected her. But, she worried about what most Egyptians thought. Did it worry them to have a woman on the throne?

If a male pharaoh was what the citizens wanted, she would act more like a man. She told everyone that her father had picked her to be pharaoh. Then, she began to change the way she looked.

The royal artists were told to paint her as a man. In pictures, she is shown wearing a short skirt called a kilt. That was the way Egyptian men dressed. Women wore long dresses.

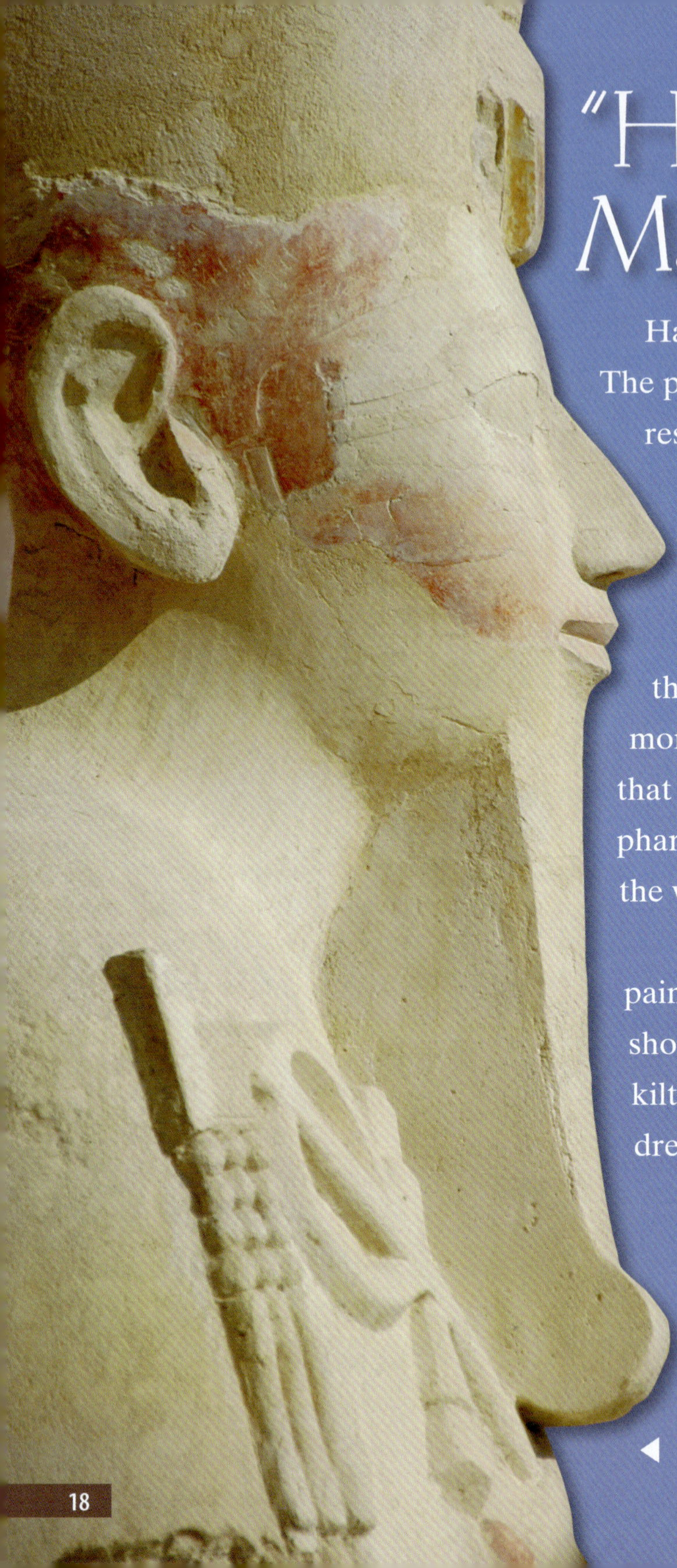

◀ This sculpture shows the fake beard.

Around her neck she wore a king's wide collar. And, on her chin, she attached a false golden beard. Hatshepsut thought the people would respect her more if she looked like a man.

Senenmut ▶ holding Princess Neferure

Hatshepsut's Size

From pictures and other facts about her, Egyptologists have learned that Hatshepsut was tiny and thin. This must have made it even harder for her to look like a man.

A Trusted Advisor

Hatshepsut had many scribes and wise assistants. Her favorite of these was a man named Senenmut (suh-nen-MOOT). He was an **architect**. As he became more important, Hatshepsut put him in charge of her building projects.

A Tale of Godly Birth

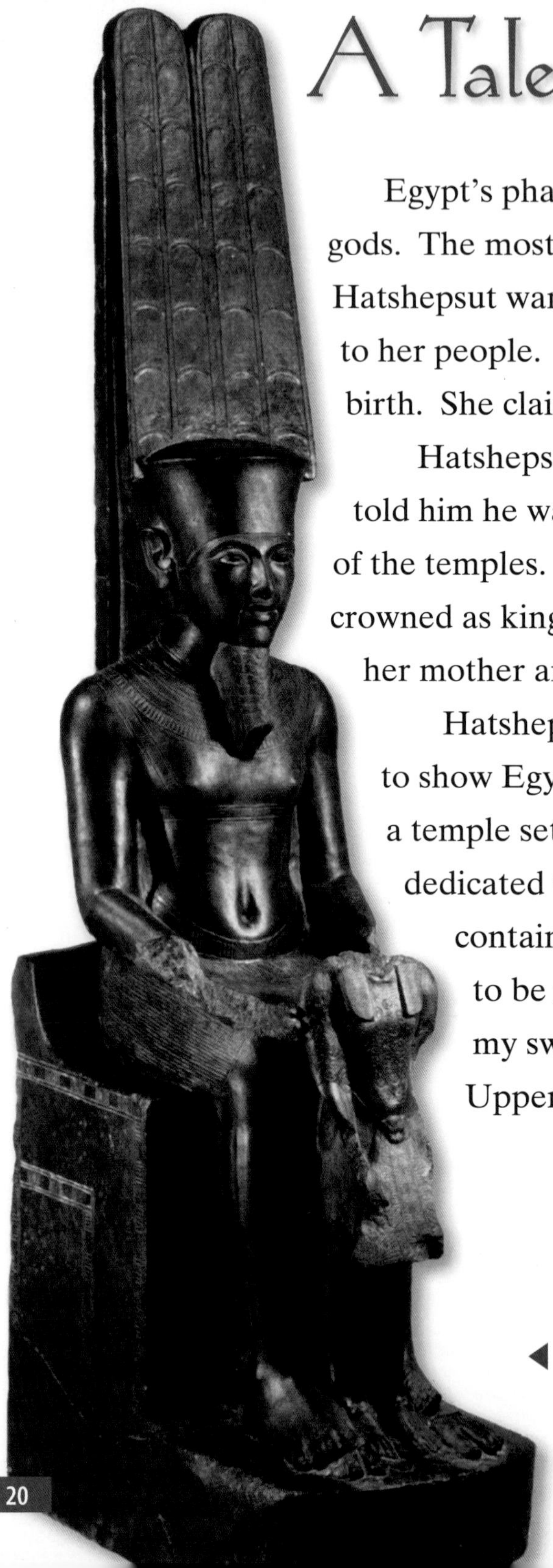

Egypt's pharaohs claimed to be related to the gods. The most important god was Amun (AH-muhn). Hatshepsut wanted to make herself more important to her people. So, she told a special story about her birth. She claimed that her father was Amun.

Hatshepsut went to her architect, Senenmut. She told him he was to create carved pictures on the walls of the temples. These images should show her being crowned as king of Egypt. The carvings also showed her mother and Amun.

Hatshepsut had workers build monuments to show Egypt's power. The largest of these was a temple set into the side of a mountain. It was dedicated to the god Amun. A wall at this temple contains hieroglyphs. The words are supposed to be from Amun. They begin: "Welcome, my sweet daughter, my favorite, the king of Upper and Lower Egypt . . ."

◀ Amun was an important god to the Egyptians.

▲ Hatshepsut's Deir el-Bahri Temple

Obelisks are seen all over Egypt today. ▶

A Temple with a Purpose

The temple Hatshepsut built in honor of Amun was in a place called Deir el-Bahri (DARE el-BAH-ree).

The Obelisks of Hatshepsut

While she was still regent, Hatshepsut ordered two large **obelisks** (AWB-uh-lisks). These were tall, thin stone columns. They tapered at the top to a peak. Their tops were covered in gold foil to make them sparkle in the sun. Hieroglyphs were carved up and down the side of the obelisks. These symbols told about the greatness of the pharaoh.

A Bold Trading Plan

▲ This map shows how the Egyptians traveled to Punt.

When Hatshepsut had been pharaoh for nine years, she sent a group of traders on a mission. They needed to go to a faraway land called Punt. The Egyptians needed a rare and expensive perfume. The perfume was called **myrrh** (MUHR). Egyptians used myrrh in their religious ceremonies. It grew on a tree that was not found in Egypt.

Hatshepsut had a huge ship built for the trip. This ship sailed south on the Nile River. Then, it was carried to the Red Sea. The waters of the Red Sea were much rougher than the Nile.

Myrrh ▶

Two years went by, and Hatshepsut had not heard from her traders. At last, they returned. Hatshepsut was thrilled to see the treasures they brought. There were perfumes and gold. They brought live panthers and leopards. A giraffe, several monkeys, and baboons were on the ship. The traders even brought back a few of the citizens of Punt.

Hatshepsut was proud of the successful trading trip. The traders also brought back 31 myrrh trees. The trees were planted in Egypt.

Where Was Punt?

History does not tell the exact location of the land of Punt. It was probably somewhere in eastern Africa, perhaps where Eritrea (er-uh-TREE-uh) is now.

Linking the Waters?

In earlier years, the Egyptians had dug a canal from the Nile River to the Red Sea. Over time, yearly flooding had filled most of the canal. That is why the traders had to carry their ship and the goods over land.

▼ This is a model of an Egyptian ship.

Trouble Over the Throne

Thutmose III was just a baby when he was crowned pharaoh. Even though he and Hatshepsut ruled together, his role was always in the background. Then, as a young man, he led Egypt's armies.

Egyptologists do not know if Thutmose III and Hatshepsut even liked each other. Thutmose may have wanted the job of pharaoh for himself. Hatshepsut probably thought she deserved the job. She would not have wanted Thutmose III taking it from her.

Hatshepsut ruled Egypt for about 22 years. When she died, she was probably in her forties.

◄ Thutmose III

After her death, Thutmose III had the crown of Egypt to himself. History shows that he was a successful and popular pharaoh. He ruled for about 30 years.

Acts of Destruction

Twenty years after her death, someone tried to have Hatshepsut erased from history. Her statues were pulled down and smashed. Pictures of her were gouged out of the scenes carved on temple walls (above). Some historians think that Thutmose III ordered the destruction. Others disagree. They do not think that he would have waited 20 years if he wanted to erase her image.

How Long Did an Egyptian Live?

Men and women in Hatshepsut's time did not live as long as people do today. If an Egyptian lived to be 40 years old, that was a long life.

▼ Most of Egypt's ruins are damaged. But, the damage to Hatshepsut's images is especially bad.

The Tomb of Hatshepsut

Egyptians believed that when they died they joined the gods. They were very careful when they planned their burial places. They arranged to have their bodies wrapped as mummies. And, they wanted to be buried with their finest treasures.

Earlier in Egypt's history, pharaohs built pyramids as their tombs. Pyramids were no longer built in Hatshepsut's time. Instead, pharaohs chose beautiful spots. There, they built stone tombs.

Hatshepsut planned for her death during her entire **reign** (RAIN). She had a huge funeral temple

◀ Mummies were put in gold caskets.

▼ Tombs in the Valley of the Kings

▲ The Temple of Deir el-Bahri

built. It was called Deir el-Bahri. It was across the Nile River from Thebes.

It was built into the cliffs and had huge columns. Deir el-Bahri contained dozens of statues and the walls were filled with hieroglyphs.

Hatshepsut also chose a secret burial place in the Valley of the Kings. Her actual mummy was placed there. That way, it was safe from grave robbers.

Deir el-Bahri Today

Visitors to Egypt can visit the temple at Deir el-Bahri. Even though much of its art was smashed, most of it has been partly restored.

The Architect

Senenmut was Hatshepsut's trusted advisor and architect. He was the designer of the temple at Deir el-Bahri. He later built himself a tomb nearby.

Leading Egypt

Sadly, Hatshepsut's mummy was not left in peace. Hundreds of years ago, thieves broke into her burial place. Her body has never been found.

Hatshepsut might not have believed that her story would last forever. She had done what no woman had ever done before. She had ruled for many years. She had built more monuments and works of art than any queen of Egypt. And she had ruled the most powerful civilization of her time.

▼ Funerals were very important to Egyptians. This image shows a funeral boat being carried.

▲ Hieroglyphs tell Egypt's story.

▲ Women in Egypt

A Plan to Become Famous

Hatshepsut built many large stone buildings. She put hieroglyphs on all their walls. These were like large billboards. She bragged about all the things she had done. She wanted people to realize how much she deserved to be king.

Women's Rights

Women in Egypt had many more rights than those in places like ancient Mesopotamia (mes-uh-puh-TAY-mee-uh) and Greece. As in many countries today, they could own property, inherit property from their parents or husbands, and even sue another person in a court of law.

Glossary

architect—a person who designs buildings

artifact—any object made by humans that belongs to an earlier time or culture

civilization—a society that has writing and keeps track of records

double crown—a half-red, half-white crown worn by Egypt's pharaohs; symbolized the union of Upper Egypt and Lower Egypt

Egyptologists—historians who study the events and culture of Egypt

hieroglyphs—pictures or symbols representing words, syllables, or sounds, used by the ancient Egyptians instead of alphabetical writing

mummy—a dead body that has been well-preserved

myrrh—a bitter-tasting African plant used to make perfume and incense

obelisks—tall, slender, four-sided pillars tapering toward pyramid tops

pharaoh—the title of a king of ancient Egypt

regent—someone who acts in the place of a king or ruler

reign—the years that a ruler is in power

scribes—people employed to record documents and copy manuscripts before the invention of printing

Index

Image Credits

cover Walter Daran/Time Life Pictures/Getty Images; p.1 Walter Daran/Time Life Pictures/Getty Images; p.4 The Granger Collection, New York; pp.4–5 Altrendo Panoramic/Getty Images; p.5 SuperStock, Inc.; p.6 Teacher Created Materials; p.7 (top) Connors Bros./Shutterstock, Inc.; p.7 (bottom) Vladimir Pomortzeff/Shutterstock, Inc.; p.8 age fotostock/SuperStock; p.9 Connors Bros./Shutterstock, Inc.; pp.10–11 Juriah Mosin/Shutterstock, Inc.; p.11 (top) The Granger Collection, New York; p.11 (bottom) Discovery Channel/Getty Images; p.12 SuperStock, Inc.; p.13 WH Chow/Shutterstock, Inc.; p.14 Teacher Created Materials; p.15 (top) The Granger Collection, New York; p.15 (bottom) The Granger Collection, New York; p.16 Teacher Created Materials; pp.16–17 Andre Klaassen/Shutterstock, Inc.; p.17 Vova Pomortzeff/Shutterstock, Inc.; p.18 Vova Pomortzeff/Shutterstock, Inc.; p.19 The Granger Collection, New York; p.20 The Granger Collection, New York; p.21 (top) Photos.com; p.21 (bottom) Carlos Arguelles/Shutterstock, Inc.; p.22 Teacher Created Materials; pp.22–23 Neil Fletcher & Matthew Ward/Getty Images; p.23 Courtesy of Larry and Valerie Lapucia; p.24 The Granger Collection, New York; p.25 (top) http://www.egyptarchive.co.uk; p.25 (bottom) The Library of Congress; p.26 (top) Scott Rothstein/Shutterstock, Inc.; p.26 (bottom) Bartlomiej K. Kwieciszewski/Shutterstock, Inc.; p.27 Corbis; p.28 Vladimir Pomortzeff/Shutterstock, Inc.; p.29 (top) Pierdelune/Shutterstock, Inc.; p.29 (bottom) Pixoi Ltd./Alamy; back cover Corbis